John Thompson's Modern Course for the Piano   FIRST GRADE

CHRISTMAS PIANO SOLOS

ISBN 978-1-4234-5689-6

WILLIS MUSIC

EXCLUSIVELY DISTRIBUTED BY

HAL•LEONARD®

7777 W. BLUEMOUND RD. P.O. BOX 13819 MILWAUKEE, WI 53213

Visit Hal Leonard Online at
www.halleonard.com

Contents

Jingle Bells

Use with John Thompson's Modern Course for the Piano FIRST GRADE BOOK, after page 6.

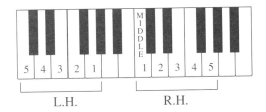

Words and Music by
J. Pierpont
Arranged by Carolyn Miller

With energy!

Jin - gle bells,   jin - gle bells,   jin - gle all the

way.   Oh, what fun it   is to ride in a

Accompaniment (Student plays one octave higher than written.)

Jolly Old St. Nicholas

Use after page 12.

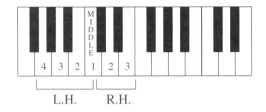

L.H.   R.H.

Traditional 19th Century American Carol
Arranged by Carolyn Miller

Happily

Jol - ly old Saint Nich - o - las, lean your ear this

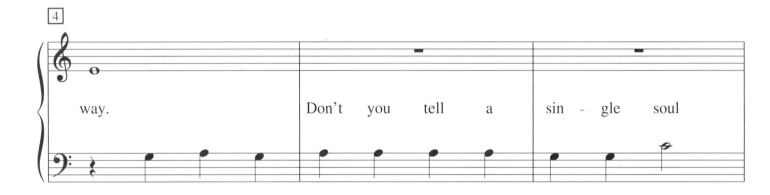

way.   Don't you tell a sin - gle soul

Accompaniment (Student plays one octave higher than written.)

Happily

7

Blue Christmas

Use after page 15.

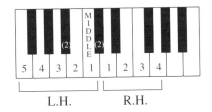

Words and Music by Billy Hayes
and Jay Johnson
Arranged by Carolyn Miller

I'll have a blue Christ- mas with - out you.

I'll be so blue think - ing a - bout you. ____

Accompaniment (Student plays one octave higher than written.)

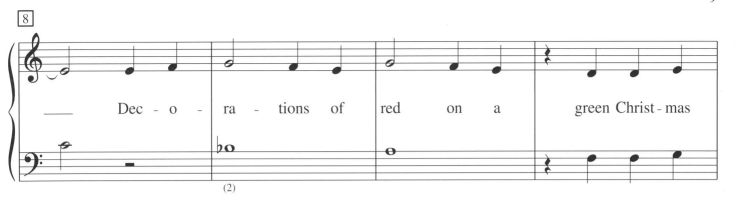

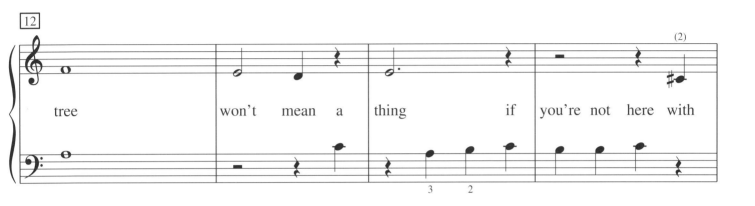

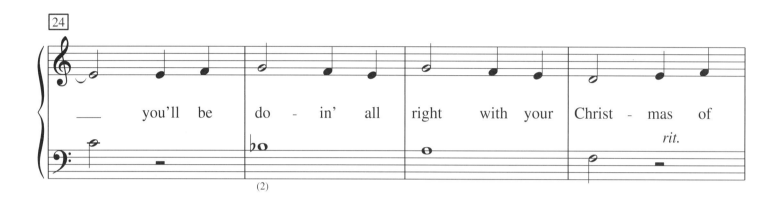

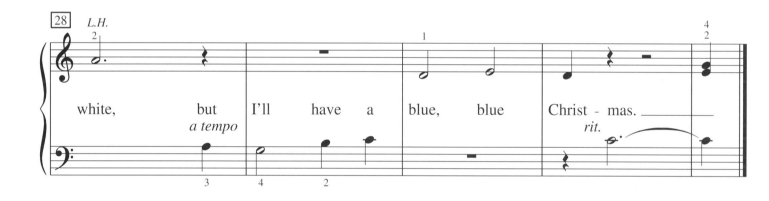

(There's No Place Like)
Home for the Holidays
Use after page 25.

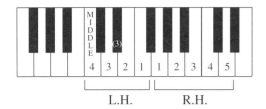

Words by Al Stillman
Music by Robert Allen
Arranged by Carolyn Miller

With feeling

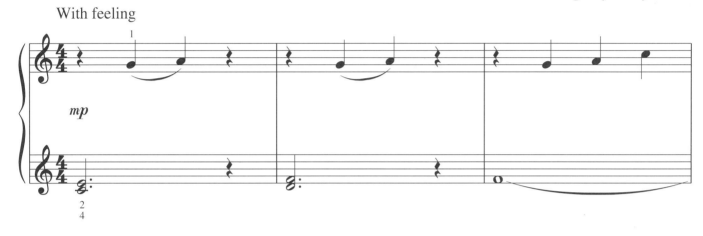

Oh, there's   no   place like   home   for   the

Accompaniment (Student plays one octave higher than written.)

With feeling

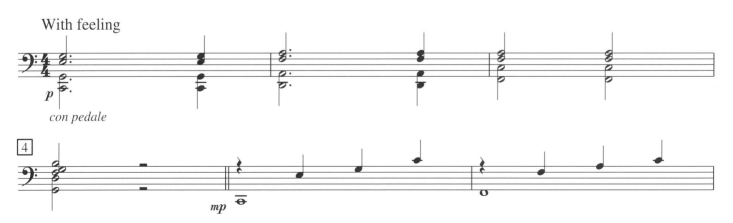

con pedale

Do You Hear What I Hear

Use after page 33.

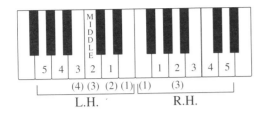

Words and Music by Noel Regney
and Gloria Shayne
Arranged by Carolyn Miller

Accompaniment (Student plays one octave higher than written.)

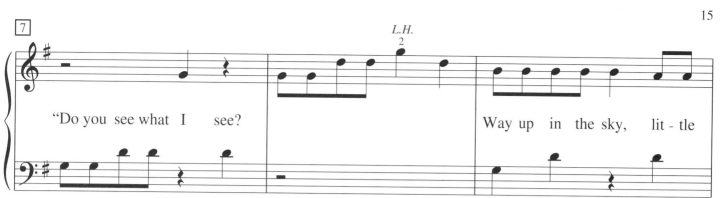

"Do you see what I see?

Way up in the sky, lit - tle

lamb.

Do you see what I see?

A

star, ___ a star

danc-ing in the night, with a

tail as big as a

kite,   with a tail as big as a kite."

Silver and Gold

Use after page 44.

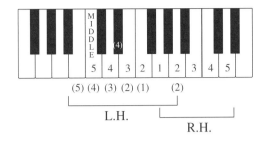

Music and Lyrics by
Johnny Marks
Arranged by Carolyn Miller

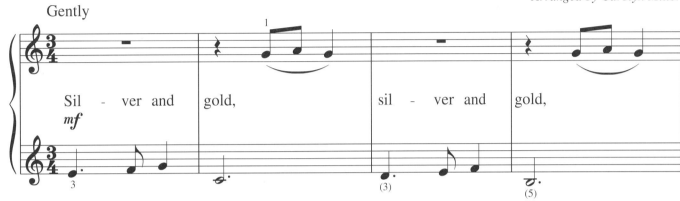

Sil - ver and gold,   sil - ver and gold,

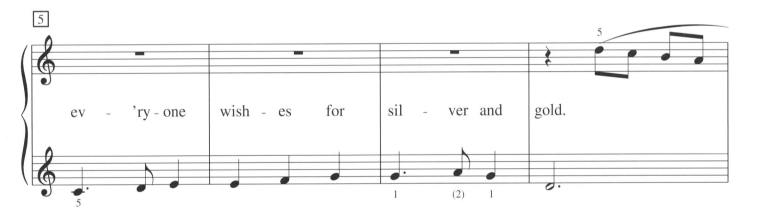

ev - 'ry - one   wish - es   for   sil - ver and gold.

Accompaniment (Student plays one octave higher than written.)

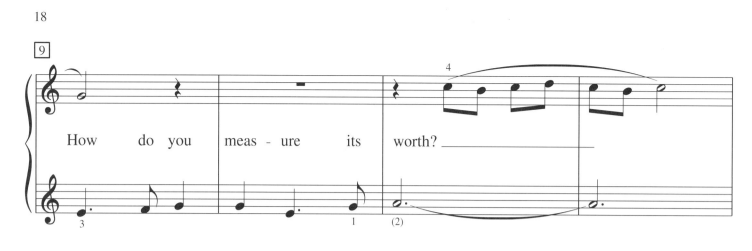

How do you meas - ure its worth? _____

Just by the pleas - ure it gives here on earth?

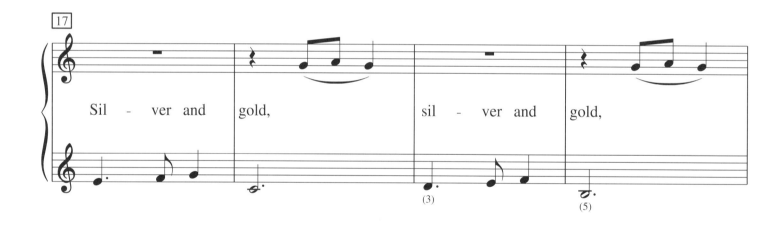

Sil - ver and gold, sil - ver and gold,

Caroling, Caroling

Use after page 48.

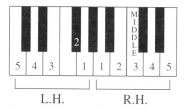

Play one octave higher for solo; play two octaves higher for duet.

Words by Wihla Hutson
Music by Alfred Burt
Arranged by Carolyn Miller

Merrily, with a lilt

Car - ol - ing, car - ol - ing, now we go; Christ - mas bells are ring - ing!

Car - ol - ing, car - ol - ing through the snow; Christ - mas bells are ring - ing!

Accompaniment (Student plays two octaves higher than written.)

Merrily, with a lilt

21

Rudolph the Red-Nosed Reindeer

Use after page 53.

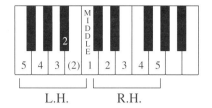

Music and Lyrics by
Johnny Marks
Arranged by Carolyn Miller

Slowly, ad lib*

You know Dash-er and Danc-er and Pranc-er and Vix-en, Com-et and Cu-pid and

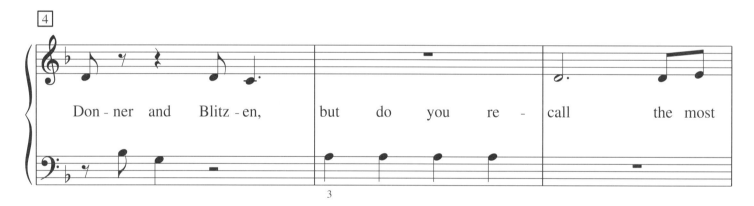

Don-ner and Blitz-en, but do you re-call the most

Ad lib (or *ad libitum*) is Latin for "at will." Play this opening section freely: imagine no barlines.

Accompaniment (Student plays one octave higher than written.)

Slowly, ad lib

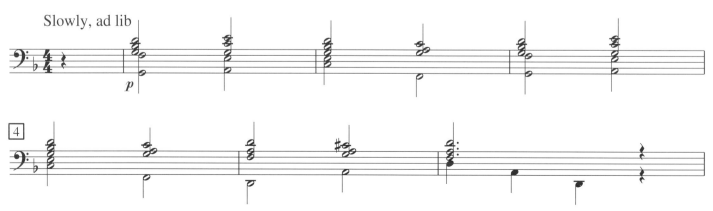

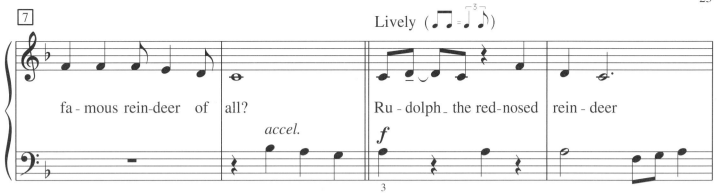

used to laugh and call him names. They nev - er let poor Ru - dolph

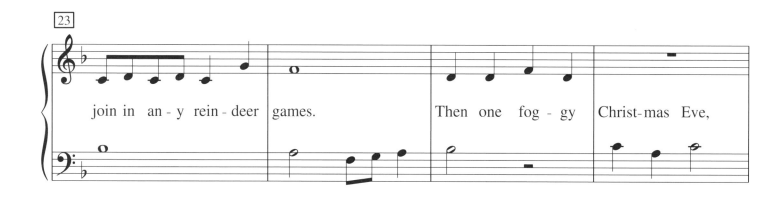

join in an - y rein - deer games. Then one fog - gy Christ - mas Eve,

San - ta came to say: "Ru - dolph, with your nose so bright, _

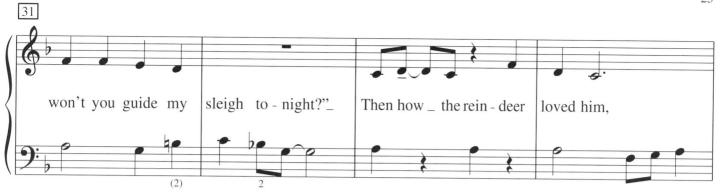

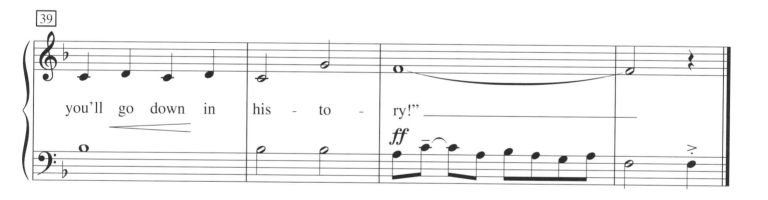

Silver Bells

from the Paramount Picture THE LEMON DROP KID

Use after page 67.

Words and Music by Jay Livingston
and Ray Evans
Arranged by Carolyn Miller

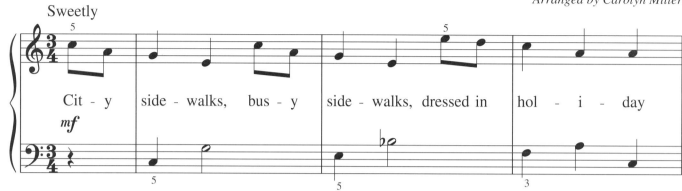

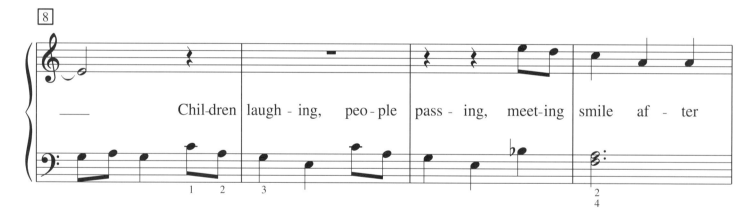

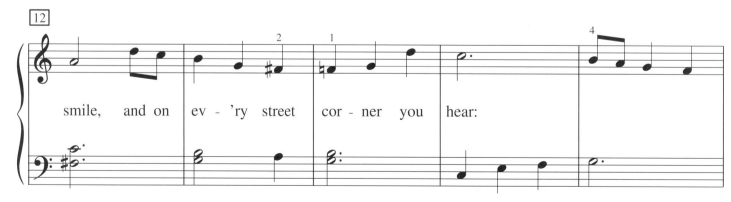

Sil - ver bells, _____ sil - ver bells, _____

it's Christ - mas time in the cit - y. _____

Ring - a - ling, _____ hear them ring, _____

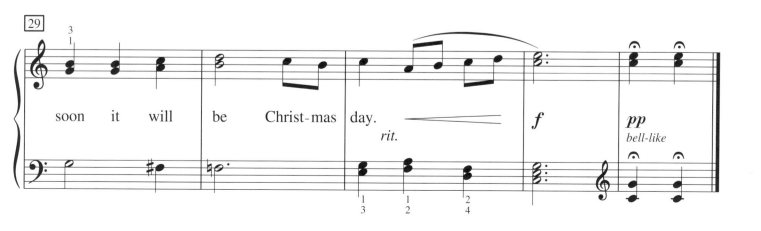

soon it will be Christ-mas day. _____ *rit.* *f* *pp* *bell-like*

Parade of the Wooden Soldiers

Use after page 74.

Music by Leon Jessel
Arranged by Carolyn Miller

Like a march

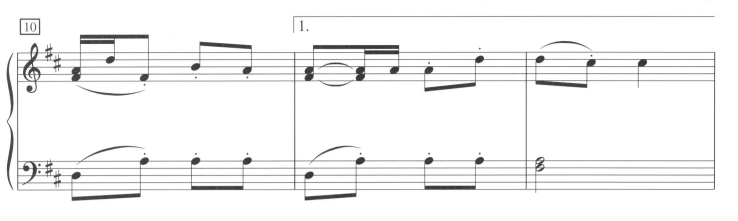

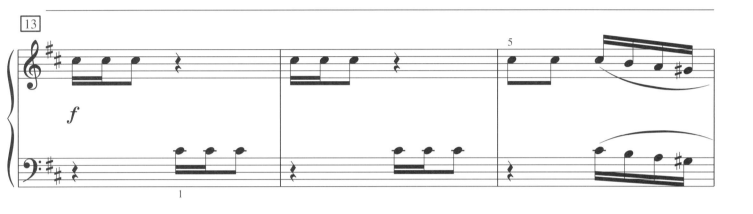

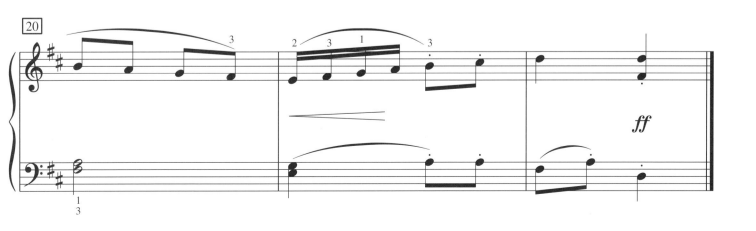

CLASSICAL PIANO SOLOS

Original Keyboard Pieces from Baroque to the 20th Century

Compiled and edited by Philip Low, Sonya Schumann, and Charmaine Siagian

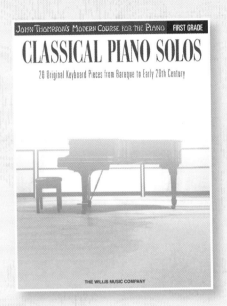

First Grade

22 pieces: *Bartók*: A Conversation • *Mélanie Bonis*: Miaou! Ronron! • *Burgmüller*: Arabesque • *Handel*: Passepied • *d'Indy*: Two-Finger Partita • *Köhler*: Andantino • *Müller*: Lyric Etude • *Ryba*: Little Invention • *Schytte*: Choral Etude; Springtime • *Türk*: I Feel So Sick and Faint, and more!
00119738 / $6.99

Second Grade

22 pieces: *Bartók*: The Dancing Pig Farmer • *Beethoven*: Ecossaise • *Bonis*: Madrigal • *Burgmüller*: Progress • *Gurlitt*: Etude in C • *Haydn*: Dance in G • *d'Indy*: Three-Finger Partita • *Kirnberger*: Lullaby in F • *Mozart*: Minuet in C • *Petzold*: Minuet in G • *Purcell*: Air in D Minor • *Rebikov*: Limping Witch Lurking • *Schumann*: Little Piece • *Schytte*: A Broken Heart, and more!
00119739 / $6.99

Third Grade

20 pieces: *CPE Bach*: Presto in C Minor • *Bach/Siloti*: Prelude in G • *Burgmüller*: Ballade • *Cécile Chaminade*: Pièce Romantique • *Dandrieu*: The Fifers • *Gurlitt*: Scherzo in D Minor • *Hook*: Rondo in F • *Krieger*: Fantasia in C • *Kullak*: Once Upon a Time • *MacDowell*: Alla Tarantella • *Mozart*: Rondino in D • *Rebikov*: Playing Soldiers • *Scarlatti*: Sonata in G • *Schubert*: Waltz in F Minor, and more!
00119740 / $7.99

Fourth Grade

18 pieces: *CPE Bach*: Scherzo in G • *Teresa Carreño*: Berceuse • *Chopin*: Prelude in E Minor • *Gade*: Little Girls' Dance • *Granados*: Valse Poetic No. 6 • *Grieg*: Arietta • *Handel*: Prelude in G • *Heller*: Sailor's Song • *Kuhlau*: Sonatina in C • *Kullak*: Ghost in the Fireplace • *Moszkowski*: Tarentelle • *Mozart*: Allegro in G Minor • *Rebikov*: Music Lesson • *Satie*: Gymnopedie No. 1 • *Scarlatti*: Sonata in G • *Telemann*: Fantasie in C, and more!
00119741 / $7.99

Fifth Grade

19 pieces: *Bach*: Prelude in C-sharp Major • *Beethoven:* Moonlight sonata • *Chopin*: Waltz in A-flat • *Cimarosa*: Sonata in E-flat • *Coleridge-Taylor*: They Will Not Lend Me a Child • *Debussy*: Doctor Gradus • *Grieg*: Troldtog • *Griffes*: Lake at Evening • *Lyadov*: Prelude in B Minor • *Mozart*: Fantasie in D Minor • *Rachmaninoff*: Prelude in C-sharp Minor • *Rameau*: Les niais de Sologne • *Schumann:* Farewell • *Scriabin*: Prelude in D, and more!
00119742 / $8.99

The *Classical Piano Solos* series offers carefully-leveled, original piano works from Baroque to the early 20th century, featuring the simplest classics in Grade 1 to concert-hall repertoire in Grade 5. An assortment of pieces are featured, including familiar masterpieces by Bach, Beethoven, Mozart, Grieg, Schumann, and Bartók, as well as several lesser-known works by composers such as Melanie Bonis, Anatoly Lyadov, Enrique Granados, Vincent d'Indy, Theodor Kullak, and Samuel Coleridge-Taylor.

• Grades 1-4 are presented in a suggested order of study. Grade 5 is laid out chronologically.

• Features clean, easy-to-read engravings with clear but minimal editorial markings.

• View complete repertoire lists of each book along with sample music pages at **www.willispianomusic.com**.

The series was compiled to loosely correlate with the *John Thompson Modern Course*, but can be used with any method or teaching situation.

A DOZEN A DAY SONGBOOK SERIES
BROADWAY, MOVIE AND POP HITS
Arranged by Carolyn Miller

The *A Dozen a Day Songbook* series contains wonderful Broadway, movie and pop hits that may be used as companion pieces to the memorable technique exercises in the *A Dozen a Day* series. They are also suitable as supplements for ANY method!

Mini
Early Elementary

A DOZEN A DAY SONGBOOK

Broadway, Movie and Pop Hits
Any Dream Will Do • Can You Feel the Love Tonight • A Dream Is a Wish Your Heart Makes
Heigh-Ho • I'm Popeye the Sailor Man • It's a Grand Night for Singing • Lean on Me
Love Me Tender • So Long, Farewell • You'll Never Walk Alone

THE WILLIS MUSIC COMPANY

MINI
LATER ELEMENTARY
Songs in the Mini Book:
Any Dream Will Do • Can You Feel the Love Tonight • A Dream Is a Wish Your Heart Makes • Heigh-Ho • I'm Popeye the Sailor Man • It's a Grand Night for Singing • Lean on Me • Love Me Tender • So Long, Farewell • You'll Never Walk Alone.

00416858 Book Only $7.99
00416861 Book/Audio $12.99

PREPARATORY
MID-ELEMENTARY
Songs in the Preparatory Book:
The Bare Necessities • Do-Re-Mi • Getting to Know You • Heart and Soul • Little April Shower • Part of Your World • The Surrey with the Fringe on Top • Swinging on a Star • The Way You Look Tonight • Yellow Submarine.

00416859 Book Only $7.99
00416862 Book/Audio $12.99

BOOK 1
LATER ELEMENTARY
Songs in Book 1:
Cabaret • Climb Ev'ry Mountain • Give a Little Whistle • If I Were a Rich Man • Let It Be • Rock Around the Clock • Twist and Shout • The Wonderful Thing About Tiggers • Yo Ho (A Pirate's Life for Me) • Zip-A-Dee-Doo-Dah.

00416860 Book Only $7.99
00416863 Book/Audio $12.99

BOOK 2
EARLY INTERMEDIATE
Songs in Book 2:
Hallelujah • I Dreamed A Dream • I Walk the Line • I Want to Hold Your Hand • In the Mood • Moon River • Once Upon A Dream • This Land is Your Land • A Whole New World • You Raise Me Up.

00119241 Book Only $6.99
00119242 Book/Audio $12.99

Prices, content, and availability subject to change without notice.

CLASSIC PIANO REPERTOIRE

The *Classic Piano Repertoire* series includes popular as well as lesser-known pieces from a select group of composers out of the Willis piano archives. Every piece has been newly engraved and edited with the aim to preserve each composer's original intent and musical purpose.

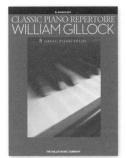

WILLIAM GILLOCK – ELEMENTARY

8 Great Piano Solos

Dance in Ancient Style • Little Flower Girl of Paris • On a Paris Boulevard • Rocking Chair Blues • Sliding in the Snow • Spooky Footsteps • A Stately Sarabande • Stormy Weather.

00416957 ....$8.99

EDNA MAE BURNAM – ELEMENTARY

8 Great Piano Solos

The Clock That Stopped • The Friendly Spider • A Haunted House • New Shoes • The Ride of Paul Revere • The Singing Cello • The Singing Mermaid • Two Birds in a Tree.

00110228 ....$8.99

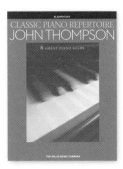

JOHN THOMPSON – ELEMENTARY

9 Great Piano Solos

Captain Kidd • Drowsy Moon • Dutch Dance • Forest Dawn • Humoresque • Southern Shuffle • Tiptoe • Toy Ships • Up in the Air.

00111968 ....$8.99

LYNN FREEMAN OLSON – EARLY TO LATER ELEMENTARY

14 Great Piano Solos

Caravan • Carillon • Come Out! Come Out! (Wherever You Are) • Halloween Dance • Johnny, Get Your Hair Cut! • Jumping the Hurdles • Monkey on a Stick • Peter the Pumpkin Eater • Pony Running Free • Silent Shadows • The Sunshine Song • Tall Pagoda • Tubas and Trumpets • Winter's Chocolatier.

00294722 ....$9.99

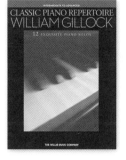

WILLIAM GILLOCK – INTERMEDIATE TO ADVANCED

12 Exquisite Piano Solos

Classic Carnival • Etude in A Major (The Coral Sea) • Etude in E Minor • Etude in G Major (Toboggan Ride) • Festive Piece • A Memory of Vienna • Nocturne • Polynesian Nocturne • Sonatina in Classic Style • Sonatine • Sunset • Valse Etude.

00416912 .... $12.99

EDNA MAE BURNAM – INTERMEDIATE TO ADVANCED

13 Memorable Piano Solos

Butterfly Time • Echoes of Gypsies • Hawaiian Leis • Jubilee! • Longing for Scotland • Lovely Senorita • The Mighty Amazon River • Rumbling Rumba • The Singing Fountain • Song of the Prairie • Storm in the Night • Tempo Tarantelle • The White Cliffs of Dover.

00110229 .... $12.99

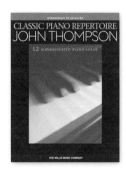

JOHN THOMPSON – INTERMEDIATE TO ADVANCED

12 Masterful Piano Solos

Andantino (from Concerto in D Minor) • The Coquette • The Faun • The Juggler • Lagoon • Lofty Peaks • Nocturne • Rhapsody Hongroise • Scherzando in G Major • Tango Carioca • Valse Burlesque • Valse Chromatique.

00111969 .... $12.99

LYNN FREEMAN OLSON – EARLY TO MID-INTERMEDIATE

13 Distinctive Piano Solos

Band Wagon • Brazilian Holiday • Cloud Paintings • Fanfare • The Flying Ship • Heroic Event • In 1492 • Italian Street Singer • Mexican Serenade • Pageant Dance • Rather Blue • Theme and Variations • Whirlwind.

00294720 ....$9.99

WILLIS MUSIC

EXCLUSIVELY DISTRIBUTED BY

HAL•LEONARD®

CLOSER LOOK View sample pages and hear audio excerpts online at www.halleonard.com

 www.willispianomusic.com

www.facebook.com/willispianomusic

Prices, content, and availability subject to change without notice.